The 7th Day, The Final Act of Creation

by

James Madison McCauley 3rd

AB ASPECT Books
www.ASPECTBooks.com

Copyright © 2016 James Madison McCauley 3rd

Copyright © 2016 Aspect Books, Inc.

ISBN-13: 978-1-4796-0700-6 (Paperback)

ISBN-13: 978-1-4796-0701-3 (ePub)

ISBN-13: 978-1-4796-0702-0 (Mobi)

Library of Congress Control Number: 2016912199

AB **ASPECT Books**
www.ASPECTBooks.com

The 7th Day
The Final Act of Creation
IV

Remember the sabbath day, to keep it holy. Six days shalt thou labour, and do all thy work: But the seventh day is the Sabbath of the LORD thy God: in it thou shalt not do any work, thou, nor thy son, nor thy daughter, thy manservant, nor thy maidservant, nor thy cattle, nor thy stranger that is within thy gates: For in six days the Lord made heaven and earth, the sea, and all that in them is, and rested the seventh day: wherefore the Lord blessed the sabbath day, and hallowed it. Exod. 20:8-11.

References

Marilyn Hickey Ministries
Denver, Colorado
Used by Permission

Dictionary of the Christian Church
Hendrickson Publishers, Inc.
P.O. Box 3473
Peabody, Massachusetts 01961-3473
© 1977 Oxford University Press
Used by permission
All Rights Reserved

All Scripture references KJV

Rights to use KJV in the United Kingdom
Permissions Department Cambridge
   University Press
University Printing House
Shaftesbury Road
Cambridge CB2 8BS
United Kingdom
Use by permission

Unpublished work © 2015 by
   James Madison McCauley 3rd
All Rights Reserved

Table of Contents

Foreword

I thank God for His mercy toward me and the revelation of the Sabbath covenant. The book is dedicated to our Lord Jesus, who faced death, and obtained the victory over it by the resurrection from the dead by the Spirit of holiness. The keeping of the seventh day Sabbath is a personal relationship between God and you. His blessing is bestowed for faithful observance. This biblical based teaching will show that neither Jesus nor His disciples changed the holy convocation and that it remains to be the 7th day. God foreseeing the breach of the Sabbath promises restoration, beginning with the house of Jacob. The angelic call is for man to worship the Creator in his admonition to repent. Grace to you, and peace, from God our Father, His Holy Spirit, and our Lord Jesus Christ, Amen.

Chapter 1 –
Creating the 7th Day

David states that God chose Moses to reveal His ways unto the Children of Israel, Ps. 103:7; Nehemiah concurs. Neh. 9:13, 14. Moses reveals that the final act of creation was the glorification of the seventh day.

Genesis 2:1-3, "Thus the heavens and the earth were finished, and all the host of them. And on the seventh day God ended his work which he had made; and he rested on the seventh day from all his work which he had made. And God blessed the seventh day, and sanctified it: because that in it he had rested from all his work which God created and made."

Jesus refers to the rest as the Sabbath, which was made for man. Mark 2:27. The record reflects that God created/worked six days and He rested the 7th day. God arose from His rest and blessed the 7th day and sanctified it. In blessing the 7th day, God spoke favor upon it causing His divine nature to rest upon the day by the impartation of holiness. "Ye shall keep the sabbath therefore: for it is holy unto you." Exod. 31:14. God proclaims the 7th day to be: "My holy day; the holy of the Lord." Isa. 58:13. God also sanctifies the 7th day making it pure and sacred, which caused His glory to rest upon the day itself. This affords the day special respect, honor, and dignity, to hold in adoration, and to be revered as holy. The command from the mouth of God is, "Remember the sabbath day to keep it holy." Exod. 20:8. Because the holiness of God rests upon the 7th day, He hallowed the day, Exod. 20:11, i.e., dedicates and devotes by setting it apart for His worship from man as God's religious day, Lev. 23:3.

Because of God's blessing upon the 7th day, each weekly occurrence is blessed, sanctified, and hallowed since its inception from the foundation of the world.

Chapter 2 –
Sabbath Made known

The first scriptural account when God commands man to rest on the Sabbath is, Exod. 16:1-30. This is when He provided the Children of Israel with manna to eat in the morning, and in the evening He gave them quail to eat. Exod. 16:12, 13.

Each person was told to gather an homer (about 2 qts.) for himself daily. Exod. 16:16. When the 6th day had begun, they were instructed to gather two homers each for consumption, for on the 7th day there would not be any manna to gather or find. Exod. 16:5, 22, 25.

When the 7th day had arrived, some of them went to pick up manna, but did not find it in the fields. Exod. 16:27. Because they had disobeyed Moses' instructions, the Lord scolded them and He commanded them to abide in their dwellings on the Sabbath. Exod. 16:28, 29. The people obeyed God and rested the 7th day according to the command. Exod. 16:30.

The record shows that Moses first refers to the 7th day as the rest of the holy Sabbath unto the Lord. Exod. 16:23. Secondly, Moses refers to the 7th day as the Sabbath unto the Lord. Exod. 16:25. Thirdly, He calls the 7th day the Sabbath. Exod. 16:26.

The reason why God had placed the Children of Israel under these commands was to see if they would walk in His law or not. Exod. 16:4. When they had arrived at Mt. Sinai, God gave them His law, 10 Commandments to live by in their service to God, and to their fellow man.

Chapter 3 –
Sabbath Law

The Lord God Almighty descends in fire upon Mt. Sinai, Exod. 19:16-18, to speak the 10 Commandments, Exod. 20:1-17, to the Children of Israel. This exhortation is of the 4th Commandment, Exod. 20:8-11, "Remember the sabbath day to keep it holy. Six days shalt thou labour, and do all thy work. But the seventh day is the sabbath (rest) of the Lord thy God: in it thou shalt not do any work, thou, nor thy son, nor thy daughter, thy manservant, nor thy maidservant, nor thy cattle, nor thy stranger that is within thy gates: for in six days the Lord made heaven and earth, the sea, and all that in them is, and rested the seventh day: wherefore the Lord blessed the sabbath day and hallowed it."

The 7th Day, The Final Act of Creation

With each occurrence of the 7th day, all people are commanded to keep it holy. Man is commanded to work 6 days and rest from his labor on the 7th day as God did from His. Heb. 4:10. By resting according to the command, man is thereby refreshed. Exod. 23:12. This Sabbath observance of God's rest of the 7th day is still relevant to the life of each Christian. Heb. 4:9-11. See Luke 23:56. In understanding the eternal significance of the commandment, its longevity is emphatically clear, "But the seventh day is the sabbath of the Lord thy God." "Heaven and earth shall pass away, but my words shall not pass away." Matt. 24:35; see also Matt. 5:18; Luke 16:17.

Chapter 4 –
Sabbath Covenant

Let us examine the Sabbath Covenant spoken by God to Moses on Mt. Sinai, prior to giving him the 10 Commandments. Exod. 31:12-17, "And the Lord spake unto Moses, saying, speak thou also unto the Children of Israel, saying, Verily my Sabbaths ye shall keep: for it is a sign between me and you throughout your generations; that ye may know that I am the Lord that doth sanctify you: ye shall keep the sabbath therefore; for it is holy unto you: every one that defileth it shall surely be put to death: for whosoever doeth any work therein, that soul shall be cut off from among his people. Six days may work be done; but in the seventh is the sabbath of rest, holy to the Lord: whosoever doeth any work in the sabbath day, he shall surely be put to death. Wherefore the Children of Israel shall keep the sabbath, to observe the sabbath throughout their generations, for a perpetual covenant. It is a sign between me and the Children of Israel for ever: for in six days the Lord made heaven and earth, and on the seventh day he rested, and was refreshed."

The covenant terms begin with a direct command, verily my Sabbaths ye shall keep. Then God explains why we are to keep it because it is an identifying mark or seal (sign) between God and man given to our understanding that in the administrative work of the Holy Spirit, He is sanctifying you. This means that God is making you holy. To sanctify is to make holy; or purify, which is to be associated with His divine power and made sacred. He says it is to be an ongoing process throughout your generations. Since the generations of man are still occurring the observance of keeping the Sabbath is still required. Mark 2:27; Heb. 4:9-11. God reminds them of His blessing upon the 7th day by stating they were to keep the Sabbath because it is holy.

God commands: every one that defileth it shall surely be put to death. To defile is to corrupt, show disrespect toward God by being irreverent or contemptuous concerning Sabbath observation, or disregard, annul its precepts as if it did not exist, or unworthy of respect, or not believe what God commanded concerning His Sabbath. See Num. 14:20-39; Ps. 78:5-11; 78:37; 95:7-11; Ezek. 20:1-26, Heb. 3:7-19; Heb 4:1-16. The biblical record of defiling the Sabbath is found in Ezek. 20:1-26; see vs. 12,13; "Moreover also I gave them my sabbaths to be a sign between me and them, that they might know that I am the Lord that sanctify them. But the house of Israel rebelled against me in the wilderness: they walked not in my statutes, and they despised my judgments, which if a man do, he shall even live in them; and my sabbaths they greatly polluted: then I said, I would pour out my fury upon them in the wilderness, to consume them." This is why God was provoked, and why He was forced to speak against them. Their example of disobedience is given to admonish all in future generations. 1 Cor. 10:1-11; Heb. 3:7-19; Ezek. 20:1-26.

God also warns those who would work on His Sabbath day. The covenant states if someone works on the Sabbath, that soul shall be cut off from among his people, and shall surely be put to death. See Exod. 31:14, 15. The biblical example of disobedience is found in Num. 15:32-41. The man was found working on the sabbath and was brought to Moses and held. God instructed him, "The man shall be surely put to death: all the congregation shall stone him with stones without the camp," v. 35. They took him away from their camp and stoned him, and he died. God was bound by the terms of the covenant He had spoken, and executed the penalty thereof.

Because of the severe punishments for disobedience, He commands them to keep the Sabbath, to observe the Sabbath throughout their generations for a perpetual covenant, which means permanently, Exod. 31:16.

Finally, in the Sabbath covenant; God says the Sabbath observance is a sign between Him and the Children of Israel forever: the chief reason is because the Lord made heaven and earth, and on the seventh day he rested, and was refreshed. Exod. 31:17; Gen. 2:3; Exod. 20:11.

From the time God spoke it, even throughout eternity, it is to be faithfully observed each occurrence because God said 'forever.' In this life, Exod. 31:17: prior to Jesus' second coming, Matt. 24:20: during Christ's millennium reign, Ezek. 46:3: for all eternity, Isa. 66:22, 23. It is the 7th day God blessed, sanctified, and made hallowed.

Chapter 5 –
Sabbath Exhortation and Explaining Unbelief

Paul's admonition of 1 Cor. 10:1-11, is a warning against ungodly living, that we should obey God's precepts. David reveals that the Children of Israel were not stedfast in His covenant. Ps. 78:37. Ezekiel shows that as a result of unbelief, disobedience, and in defiling the Sabbath is why they were overthrown. Ezek. 20:1-26.

The Hebrews account verified why they were overthrown. Heb. 3:7-19. It exhorts all people to place their faith in God, and enter into His rest. Heb. 4:1-11, is an admonition to enter into God's rest because it remains, v. 9. God's example of working 6 days and resting the 7th day is still vital to the

Christian walk unless one would fall after the same example of unbelief, vs. 1-11. The promise in keeping the rest, v. 1, is that God will cause you to; "Ride upon the high places of the earth, and feed you with the heritage of Jacob thy father: for the mouth of the Lord hath spoken it." Isa. 58:12-14. The blessings are bestowed upon the faithful observer. See Isa. 56:1-8; Isa. 58:12-14; Deut. 28:1-14. As an example, the followers of Christ observed the Commandment of resting upon the 7th day. Luke 23:56. God desires for you to also observe the Sabbath rest, it is the will of God. This is not too difficult for you to understand, nor is it a complicated matter, nor is it so overwhelming that you cannot adjust your life to comply with the spoken word of God. #1. Do no work on the 7th day. Exod. 20:8-11. #2. Come to church. Lev. 23:1-3. #3. Do good deeds to others as the opportunity arises. Isa. 58:6,7; Matt. 12:12; 25:34-40. We obey the precepts of God as commanded by Jesus, Matt. 4:4; because He spoke them. Deut. 8:3; Exod. 20:1-17. This is the reason why, because God's word is both eternal and unchanging. Mal. 3:6; Heb. 13:8; Eccles. 3:14; Isa. 14:24, 27; 40:8; 55:11; Ps. 89:34; 119:9; 33:11; 119:89, 152, 160; 1 Pet. 1:25.

In understanding unbelief; the Children of Israel did not believe what Moses had taught them, nor heed the words God had spoken. The Bible teaches clearly that because of their rebellion and in defiling the Sabbath God consumed them in the wilderness. Ezek. 20:13. They refused to obey God and not enter into His rest as preached unto them, so their unbelief caused them to err and as a result the provocation occurred. See. Heb. 3:7-19.

Before the fall, man was created to have fellowship with God. His system of belief was faith and confidence in trusting, accepting, and believing God's word to be true. Today, we must learn to trust God, Prov. 3:5,6; and be of the opinion that in obeying His word is the right thing to do. Rev. 22:14. Paul concurs to that fact by his admonition in 1 Cor. 10:1-11, that we should obey God, 1 Cor. 7:19, and do not follow their example of unbelief and rebellion.

Solomon instructs, "Let us hear the conclusion of the whole matter: fear God, and keep his commandments: for this is the whole duty of man." Eccles. 12:13.

The Bible teaches that the rest of God, Gen. 2:1-3; was made for man, Mark 2:27; God's rest is to be observed, Exod. 20:8-11; as a perpetual covenant, Exod. 31:16; for you to worship your Creator, Lev. 23:1-3; to keep as a sign between God and you, that you may know that He is the Lord that doth sanctify you, Exod. 31:13; the Sabbath rest remains, Heb. 4:9-11; and must be observed unless you would also fall after the same example of unbelief, Heb. 4:11; the blessing is bestowed for faithful observance,

Isa. 56:1-8; 58:12-14; Deut. 28:1,2. The command from the mouth of God, Matt. 4:4, is: "Remember the sabbath day to keep it holy. Six days shalt thou labour, and do all thy work: But the seventh day is the sabbath of the Lord thy God: in it thou shalt not do any work… "Exod. 20:8-11. As a believer, it is your duty before God to observe His command in obedience, lest any man would fall after the same example of unbelief. Heb. 4:11. See in relation Matt. 19:16-19; 1 Cor. 7:19, Matt. 5:17-20; 1 John 2:3-6; Rev. 12:17; 14:12; 22:14; Ps. 19:7-11; 119.

Chapter 6 –
Sabbath is a Holy Convocation

The Word of God requires man to come before Him to worship on the 7th day. Levitical law states clearly, "And the Lord spake unto Moses, saying, speak unto the Children of Israel, and say to them, concerning the feasts of the Lord, which ye shall proclaim to be holy convocations, even these are my feasts. Six days shall work be done: but the seventh day is the sabbath of rest, an holy convocation; ye shall do no work therein: it is the sabbath of the Lord in all your dwellings." Lev. 23:1-3. "Ye shall keep my sabbaths, and reverence my sanctuary: I am the Lord." Lev. 19:30; 26:2; see Eccl. 5:1, 2.

Firstly, God calls the Sabbath, "...even these are my feasts." Lev. 23:2. A feast is a celebration, a joyful event. We celebrate our Sabbath from sunset the 6th day until sunset the 7th day. See Lev. 23:32 (in relation.) David's joyful description of Sabbath keeping and in attending church is a celebration of praise and adoration for God. Ps. 42:4; 95:1-6; 100:1-5.

Secondly, God proclaims the 7th day to be a holy convocation. Lev. 23:3. This is when He requires man to come before Him and worship Him and praise Him. It is the Sabbath of the Lord in all your dwellings, Lev. 23:3, which is everywhere upon earth. God said the Sabbath observance is a perpetual covenant. Exod. 31:16. Even during the millennium reign of Christ, all people will come to worship on the 7th day Sabbath. Ezek. 46:3, and throughout all eternity. Isa. 66:22, 23.

Your walk with God should be very similar to how Jesus walked while on earth. 1 John 2:6. Jesus observed the convocation in the tradition of the forefathers. Luke 4:16. Luke's observance of the church was recorded in the book of Acts; and about three (3) decades in observing how the church conducted itself and its mannerisms, he wrote concerning its actions. Paul kept the Sabbath convocation as his custom like Christ did. Acts 13:13-41; Acts 17:2; Acts 18:4. The Jews and Gentiles also kept the 7th day convocation. Acts. 13:42, 44. In this tradition of observance is when the Scriptures were preached. Acts 13:15; Acts 15:21; Acts 17:2; Acts 18:4; Luke 4:16-19. The traditional

Mosaic observance was to be held as they had been taught. 2 Thess. 2:15. The Jews were blessed by faithful observance of the Sabbath. Isa. 58:12-14. The Gentiles were also blessed in keeping the Sabbath. Isa. 56:1-8. When we are obedient to God's Word, it results in being blessed by God. See Deut. 28:1, 2; Acts 5:32; Rev. 22:14; Acts 10:34, 35. By Cornelius' faithfulness, God blessed him. See Acts 10:1-4, in relation to Isa. 58:6-8; Acts 5:32; Acts 10:34-48; John 14:15-27; John 16:13.

Chapter 7 –
Sabbath Blessings

Isa. 56:1-8; 58:12-14.

The hand of God bestows blessing upon those who keep the 7th day Sabbath. Isaiah's revelation prophecy in relation to faithful observance shows: "Thus saith the Lord, Keep ye judgment, and do justice: for my salvation is near to come, and my righteousness to be revealed. Blessed is the man that doeth this, and the son of man that layeth hold on it; that keepeth the Sabbath from polluting it, and keepeth his hand from doing any evil. Neither let the son of the stranger, that hath joined himself to the Lord, speak, saying, The Lord hath utterly separated me from his people: neither let the eunuch say, Behold, I am a dry tree.

Sabbath Blessings

For thus saith the Lord unto the eunuchs that keep my sabbaths, and choose the things that please me, and take hold of my covenant; even unto them will I give in mine house and within my walls a place and a name better than of sons and of daughters: I will give them an everlasting name, that shall not be cut off. Also the sons of the stranger, that join themselves to the Lord, to serve him, and to love the name of the Lord, to be his servants, every one that keepeth the Sabbath from polluting it, and taketh hold of my covenant; even them will I bring to my holy mountain, and make them joyful in my house of prayer: their burnt offerings and their sacrifices shall be accepted upon mine alter; for mine house shall be called an house of prayer for all people. The Lord God, which gathereth the outcasts of Israel saith, yet will I gather others to him, beside those that are gathered unto him."

We see that the keeping of the Sabbath is very precious to the Lord. To those who keep it, He promises to bless them, v. 2. He will give to the eunuchs a place within His walls, and give to them an everlasting name, v. 5. God also vows to bring everyone that keeps the Sabbath to His holy mountain. He will make them joyful in His house of payer, and accept their sacrifices upon His alter, vs. 6, 7. He will also give them inheritance among the Children of Israel, v. 8; Isa 56:1-8.

The 7th Day, The Final Act of Creation

Unto the house of Jacob, He promises restoration of the Sabbath through repentance, and faithful observance, giving the assurance that He will bestow upon them the heritage of Jacob.

Isa. 58:12-14; "And they that shall be of thee shall build the old waste places: thou shalt raise up the foundations of many generations; and thou shalt be called, the repairer of the breach, the restorer of paths to dwell in. If thou turn away thy foot from the Sabbath, from doing thy pleasure on my holy day; and call the Sabbath a delight, the holy of the Lord, honorable; and shalt honour him, not doing thine own ways, nor finding thine own pleasure, nor speaking thine own words: Then shalt thou delight thyself in the Lord; and I will cause thee to ride upon the high places of the earth, and feed thee with the heritage of Jacob thy father: for the mouth of the Lord hath spoken it."

Additional assurance that it is God's will for man to keep the Sabbath, and observe His holy convocation is within the angelic call to mankind to worship Him who created all. Rev. 14:6, 7.

With the prophetic revelation of blessing for those who heed God's message and worship Him in Spirit and in truth, comes the provision of God as He promises to bestow. Deut. 28:1, 2; Isa. 56:1-8; Isa. 58:12-14; Rev. 22:14; 1 Cor. 6:19; Acts 5:29-32; John 14:15-21; Ps. 119:77; Matt. 6:31-33.

Chapter 8 –
No Scriptural Change

Both Old and New Testaments authenticate the Mosaic 7th day Sabbath. With no Scriptural verification to authorize a change, the rest remains. Heb. 4:9. In today's society, there are sects and denominations which support distorted non-authentic revelations from 1st day scriptural passages in the New Testament which actually are irrelevant subordinate doctrines upholding the view that the 1st day of the week is now the day of rest. They are, in fact, false assumptions because Jesus reveals that the Scripture cannot be broken. John 10:35.

When studying or researching the Bible, its various themes are, in fact, studied line upon line, precept upon precept, here a little and there a little,

Isa. 28:10, 13. Each theme studied must correlate with other passages presenting the exact same theme to gain a correct view by the Holy Spirit's direction, John 16:13, and instruction in the way of truth, Ps. 23:1, 2.

It is factual that Jesus, Paul, the disciples, Jews, and Gentiles all observed the Mosaic Sabbath according to Levitical Law. In Acts 15:21, the Law and the Prophets were read in the synagogues every Sabbath. Jesus, as was his custom, went into the synagogues and taught. Luke 4:16-32, vs. 16, 31. While Jesus' followers kept the Sabbath rest, Luke 23:56, the disciples concur to the keeping of the Mosaic convocation in the establishment of the Gentile's covenant. Acts 15:1-32, see v. 21. Paul likewise preached in the synagogues on the Sabbath in the observance of the Levitical convocational law. See Acts 13:13-44; Acts 17:2; Acts 18:4. Jews and Gentiles alike attended the traditional convocation. Acts 13:42-44. Most of these occurrences had happened up to three decades after the ascension of our Lord Jesus Christ. Luke's writings of these accounts were around 61 A.D.

The following verses in the New Testament will be expounded to provide a correct perspective. They do not authorize change in the 7th day Sabbath observance, or change to the Levitical convocation of the 7th day.

No Scriptural Change

John 20:19; "Then the same day at evening, being the first day of the week, when the doors were shut where the disciples were assembled for fear of the Jews; came Jesus and stood in the midst, and saith unto them, peace be unto you." The correct view is that three days prior to this recorded account, the Jews had petitioned Pilate for Jesus' death, see Matthew 27. The verse reveals their fear from Jewish persecution. If you remember, when they came to arrest Jesus in the Garden of Gethsemane, they fled from the Jews. See Matt. 26:56. Peter even denies Jesus three times. Matt. 26:69-75. Jesus, knowing their fear of the Jews, comes and calms them by saying peace be unto you. Jesus shows them His hands and feet and their whole demeanor and attitudes dramatically changes from being fearful to that of joy and gladness. John 20:20; Luke 24:37-41. In this verse of Scripture there is no authorization from Christ to challenge the law, or the covenant, or the convocation; therefore, it remains to be the 7th day. In fact, the writer of Hebrews emphatically states that if Jesus had given another day of rest, he would have said so. Heb. 4:8.

Acts 20:7; "And upon the first day of the week, when the disciples came together to break bread, Paul preached unto them, ready to depart on the morrow, and continued his speech until midnight." It was the daily administrative duties of the disciples to the new converts and to believers to hold communion and preach the word. Acts 2:46, 47; 5:42; 6:1-4. Jesus had commissioned them to evangelize the world. Matt. 28:19, 20. The verse simply reveals that the disciples came together at a certain place to break bread and edify one another in the faith. Paul being moved in his compassion for his brothers in Christ was moved to speak unto them, because he would be leaving them in the morning. Paul had a habit of telling the disciples how God was working through him while he was out on the road. Acts. 14:27; 15:1-4. With the verse there is no voice of doctrinal change of the Sabbath by commandment, nor new covenant by direct command as it is in the Old Testament. In fact, God says, "My covenant will I not break, nor alter the thing that is gone out of my lips." Ps. 89:34, see also Mal. 3:6; Isa. 40:8, Luke 16:17; Matt. 5:18; Ps. 103:17, 18. With Jesus' words that the Scripture cannot be broken, John 10:35, Paul exhorts: "All Scripture is given by inspiration of God, and is profitable for doctrine, for reproof, for correct, for instruction in righteousness: that the man of God may be perfect throughly furnished unto all good works." 2 Tim. 3:16, 17. David shows that the counsel of God is everlasting. Ps. 33:11, "The counsel of the Lord standeth forever, the thoughts of his heart to all generations." Peter declares, "Knowing this first, that no prophecy of the Scripture is of any private interpretation, for the prophecy came not in old time by the will of man:

but holy men of God spake as they were moved by the Holy Ghost." 2 Pet. 1:20, 21. No change can be activated because God's Word is eternal. Heb. 13:8; 1 Pet. 1:25; Isa. 40:8; Eccles. 3:14.

1 Cor. 16:2, "Upon the first day of the week let every one of you lay by him in store, as God hath prospered him, that there be no gatherings when I come." Firstly, the passage of 1 Cor. 16:1-4, is concerning the collection of tithes and offerings for the saints and church in Jerusalem. Paul exhorts them not to be gathering when he would arrive. Paul presented himself on the Sabbath day to preach the word. Acts 13:14, 42, 44; 16:13; 17:2; 18:4. Paul says to gather on the first day in reference as being a day of work in agreement with God's instructions that the first day is a day of work. Gen. 1:1-5; Exod. 20:8-11, and according to the Commandment, to do no work on the 7th day, of which Paul instructs: "that there be no gatherings when I come." With this verse there is no factual evidence or authorization from God to produce Sabbath change.

Col. 2:16, 17, "Let no man therefore judge you in meat, or in drink, or in respect of an holy day, or of the new moon, or of the sabbath days; which are a shadow of things to come; but the body is of Christ."

Paul states to let no one judge you concerning the respect of a holy day. Their holy days are found in Leviticus chapter 23. All of which were established by God that were held as traditional occurrences in their respective seasons. During that era of time, the Gentiles who did not understand their customs, may have questioned their actions; which is probably what prompted Paul's response in that manner. Concerning the Sabbath observances, it was factual the Israelites kept the Mosaic traditional convocation of the 7th day because God had commanded them to observe it as a perpetual covenant. Exod. 31:16.

Paul also instructs the Thessalonians to likewise hold fast to the traditions which they had been taught. 2 Thess. 2:15. During that entire era of time, the keeping of the 7th day Sabbath was relevant to Christianity, the Scriptures confirm this completely. See Acts 13:14-44; 15:21; 16:13-15; 17:2; 18:4; Heb. 4:1-11.

Chapter 9 –
Change of the
Sabbath Convocation

During the 4th century, church historical records reflect a man-made law changing the day of rest from the 7th day to the 1st day. Legislation was passed in the reign of Roman Emperor Constantine, and enforced throughout the world. The Roman law under Constantine's direction required abstention from work on Sunday, and to hold Sunday as a public holiday. The observance of Sunday as the day of rest was promulgated as law and consecrated to the service of God, 321 A.D. This was regulated by both ecclesiastical and civil legislation from the 4th century. It was enjoined by the Council of Elvira in that era. See heading, "Sunday," in the *Dictionary of the Christian Church*, formerly known as the *Oxford Dictionary of the Christian Church*. Additionally, the chief reason for the substitution of Sunday for the Sabbath was the commemoration of the resurrection which was first observed by St. Ignatius. It appears that because Jesus rose from the dead on the 1st day, it gave the day its joyful character; however, the Lord gives reference to the 1st day as a day of work: Gen. 1:1-5; Exod. 20:8-11. Paul also confirms it as a day of work. 1 Cor. 16:2.

The change in times and laws by Constantine's regime seem to fit Daniel's prophecy of the 4th kingdom, which also concurs with St. John's Revelation, showing Rome as the dominant force ruling over the earth's population by legislation. See Dan. 7:1-25; Rev. 17:1-18. About three years had passed from the inauguration of Constantine's Sunday laws being 324 A.D. when he with the aid of the Council of Laodicea passed additional legislature to authorize the death of anyone caught observing the 7th day Sabbath, or Judaizing, which also fits Daniel's prophecy, "and shall wear out the saints of the most High." Dan. 7:25. According to church historian Eusebius, there was great Christian persecution during that era.

Because of the establishment of 1st day worship, this now is the predominate doctrine which is observed in most places on earth. The resurrection of Jesus is to be a lively hope in the doctrine of salvation.

Change of the Sabbath Convocation

1 Pet. 1:3; Acts 2:22-47; Rom. 1:3,5, however, it is not commanded by the living God to be His Sabbath, or His covenant, or His holy convocation. The correct order of worship is to hold convocation before God on the 7th day Sabbath. Lev. 23:1-3. This is the everlasting sign between God and man, to rest the 7th day, Exod. 20:8-11, and observe it as a perpetual convent. Exod. 31:16, 17. To violate this observance is a breach of spirit. Isaiah prophesied that this breach will be healed by keeping the 7th day Sabbath which is the correct path to dwell in. Isa. 58:12-14. God's will for those who stand in opposition to His truths is to revert and do the truth. His angels come to warn the unruly. Rev. 14:6, 7. Jesus said, "Thou shalt worship the Lord thy God, and him only shalt thou serve." Matt. 4:10. Think of this if you will: If you fail to believe the biblical precepts of the Sabbath, aren't you doing the same thing that the Children of Israel did (Heb. 3:7-19) that Paul exhorted about (1 Cor. 10:1-11) of why God overthrew them for? Ezek. 20:1-21, v. 13.

If Jesus Himself kept the Mosaic traditional Sabbath convocation as shown by Luke 4:16, then shouldn't you also follow Jesus' example since you are to pattern your life by His lifestyle, and conduct yourself accordingly? 1 John 2:6. Jesus' followers observed the rest like the Commandment requires, Luke 23:56, shouldn't you do the same? Paul kept the convocation being his custom also. Acts 17:2; 18:4, so did the Jews and the Gentiles. Acts. 13:42, 44. These recorded Sabbath meetings by Luke were written concerning the church's conduct three decades after Christ's ascension, 61 A.D., proving Scripturally that the traditional Mosaic convocation was obeyed by all of Christ's believers. Acts 13:14-44; 15:21; 16:13; 17:2; 18,4.

With diligent research by any scholar or layperson; when comparing God's law, covenant and convocational observance, to that of Constantine's rulings, we find two different sets of laws; commands, and opinions, hence, God versus man. A biblical example of non-compliance to God's law is found in 1 Kings 18:17-40. In Elijah's contest with the prophets of Baal, the Lord proved convincingly before them all, He alone is God, and that His commands are to be faithfully kept instead of man's refusal to comply with them. To obey God is the most important priority we could achieve. Elijah told King Ahab that he was serving Baal because he had forsaken the commandments of God. 1 Kings 18:18. Does this also apply to you when you forsake the Commandments of God? Think about it, what should you do as a result? Repent.

Chapter 10 –
Exhortation to Obedience

We should intently listen when God is teaching His precepts. When we read the Bible, it is the Lord speaking to us. Matt. 22:31, 32. God requires His people to observe and hallow the Sabbath by doing no work therein. Jer. 17:19-27. When we obey His precepts, we are are positioned to receive His promises and blessings, Deut. 28:1-14; Isa. 56:1-8; 58:12-14; Matt. 6:24-33; Acts 5:32; Rev. 22:14. When we disobey there are consequences. Deut. 28:15-68; Heb. 10:26-31; Numb 15:30, 31; Prov. 13:13; 2 Chron. 36:16; 1 Pet. 2:20-22. God shows admonition against rebellion in the life of Saul. 1 Sam. 15:22, 23, "And Samuel said, hath the Lord as great delight in burnt offerings and sacrifices, as in obeying the voice of the Lord? Behold, to obey is better than sacrifice, and to hearken than the fat of rams for rebellion is as the sin of witchcraft, and stubbornness is as iniquity and idolatry. Because thou hast rejected the word of the Lord, he hath also rejected thee from being king." Being obedient is what God desires for you. The passage shows the result of disobedience as being rejected, and with Christ's teaching, committing iniquity could have an adverse result. See Matt. 7:21-23. With Solomon's objective conclusion we are to fear God and keep his Commandments which is our life's duty. Eccl. 12:13. He exhorts, "Trust in the Lord with all thine heart; and lean not unto thine own understanding. In all thy ways acknowledge him, and he shall direct thy paths." Prov. 3:5, 6; Ps. 23:1, 2. We trust God by placing all of our faith, hope, trust/confidence in Him and His Word at all times. When we trust God, we will communicate our concerns with Him, for He cares for us, 1 Pet. 5:7. When you acknowledge God in all your ways, you're trusting Him to lead you in paths of righteousness. Ps. 23:1, 2. The word of the Lord is our guide as David sings, "Thy word is a lamp unto my feet, and a light unto my path." Ps. 119:105. Jesus said, "I am the light of the world: he that followeth me shall not walk in darkness, but shall have the light of life." John 8:12. When we follow Jesus, we do what the Word says. John 10:27, 28. With any issue of faith trust earnestly in the Lord as your confidence.

Exhortation to Obedience

In the teachings of Christ we view, "Thou shalt love the Lord thy God with all thy heart, and with all thy soul, and with all thy mind. This is the first and great commandment. And the second is like unto it, thou shalt love thy neighbor as thyself. On these two commandments hang all the law and the prophets." Matt. 22:37-40. If you truly love God, you will cleave to Him and be loyal from your heart toward Him in putting Him first in all things life related. Exod. 20:3. In your priorities, your deeds and service is His only with no idolatry committed by your actions. Exod. 20:4, 5. You will keep His commands out of love for Him, and then He will show you mercy. Exod. 20:6. Out of your love for God you would always reverence His holy name, and never speak it in vain because He will require it. Exod. 20:7. When you love God, you will remember His holy Sabbath day, and come to the convocation and rest from your labours, which should be your #1 priority observed in love, respect, and adoration for God. The first 4 of the 10 Commandments reflect our service to our Heavenly Father in holiness and in righteousness. Deut. 6:2; Eccl. 12:13; Ps. 19:7-14; 78:4-7; 119:1-8; 145:4, 17. The remaining 6 Commandments are observed in love toward other people, in our daily encounters with them. The man came to Jesus and said to him, "Good Master, what good thing shall I do, that I may have eternal life? And he said unto him, why callest thou me good?

There is none good but one, that is God: but if thou wilt enter into life, keep the commandments. He saith unto him, which? Jesus said, Thou shalt do no murder, thou shalt not commit adultery, thou shalt not steal, thou shalt not bear false witness, honor thy father and thy mother: and and, thou shalt love thy neighbor as thyself." Matt. 19:16-19. Paul also concurs to Christ's teaching. Rom. 13:8-10.

When we love God fully, we also love our neighbor from our heart to where our actions toward them reflect our love of God. Jesus taught, "Let your light so shine before men, that they may see your good works, and glorify your father which is in heaven." Matt. 5:16. Paul also encourages us to obey God, 1 Cor. 7:19; and to delight in the law of God after the inward man, Rom. 7:22. In faith we establish it by obeying the precepts in order to experience the bestowed blessing. Deut. 28:1, 2; Ps. 19:7-11; Exod. 20:6; Rev. 22:14. John taught, "For this is the love of God, that we keep his commandments: and his commandments are not grievous." 1 John 5:3. During the last days prior to Christ's second coming, the people of God keep His commandments, and have the testimony of Jesus Christ. Rev. 12:17. Those faithful saints keep the commandments of God, and have the faith of Jesus. Rev. 14:12. John also taught, "I have no greater joy than to hear that my children walk in truth." 3 John 4.

Exhortation to Obedience

Jesus said to His disciples, "If ye love me, keep my commandments." John 14:15, and "He that hath my commandments, and keepeth them, he it is that loveth me: and he that loveth me shall be loved of my father, and I will love him, and will manifest myself to him." John 14:21; See also Acts 5:32; Col. 1:27.

The Holy Spirit reveals, "Blessed are they that do his commandments, that they may have right to the tree of life, and may enter in through the gates into the city." Rev. 22:14. When we recall the actions of Adam and Eve, they were expelled from the Garden of Eden for disobeying God, and were prohibited from eating of the tree of life. Gen. 3:1-24. But John shows us when we obey God's Commandments, it gives us the right to eat from the tree of life. Let us make every effort to walk in obedience to His word.

Chapter 11 –
Scriptural Admonition

Paul states we are the servants of whom we obey whether of the law of sin unto death, or of obedience unto righteousness, Rom. 6:16. Sin is the transgression of the law, 1 John 3:4. David says that God will rebuke the proud who are cursed which err from His commandments, Ps. 119:21. The wages of sin is death, Rom. 6:23. Paul states we are to awake to righteousness and sin not, 1 Cor. 15:34. He says we are to keep God's commandments, 1 Cor. 7:19. Jesus is sent to us spiritually to turn us from our iniquities, Acts 3:26, and to destroy the works of the devil, 1 John 3:8. Jesus sets us free from sin, Rom. 6:22, and we do not commit sin, 1 John 3:9. But if we sin, we have an advocate with the father, 1 John 2:1, and if we confess our sins God is faithful and just to forgive us and cleanse us from all unrighteousness, 1 John 1:9. Jesus said that God is a spirit, John 4:24, and God's law is spiritual in Paul's observation, Rom. 7:14. We are to delight in the law of God after the inward man, Rom. 7:22. With our minds we serve the law of God, Rom. 7:25; 8:4-7, and meditate upon it day and night, see Josh. 1:8. We do not void the law through faith, we establish the law, Rom. 3:31. In plain terms, we obey the 10 Commandments, 1 John 2:3, 4; Matt. 19:16-19; 1 Cor. 7:19; Rev. 22:14; 12:17; 14:12.

At Jesus' return, He will send forth His angels to sever the just from among the wicked, Matt. 13:49, 50. As previously shown, the wicked are those who commit iniquity. Ps. 119:21; see also Jesus' words in Matt. 7:21-23. The very Commandment the majority of the world forgets and do not obey is the very Commandment God says to remember, Exod. 20:8-11. People tend to turn a blind eye or a deaf ear to the 4th Commandment. James informs us that whoever keeps the law but offends in one point, he is guilty of all, James 2:10. So what's wrong with this omission of the Sabbath Commandment by the majority of the world's population? It is because they are deceived by unsound doctrine, and polluted, stained by sin. Jesus said men love darkness rather than light, because their deeds were evil, John 3:19. Saul was rejected for being rebellious to God's commands, 1 Sam. 15:22, 23. The Children of Israel were overthrown in the wilderness for being rebellious, Ezek. 20:1-26; 1 Cor. 10:1-11; unbelief, Heb. 3:18. Those living in error are called by the father to repent, 2 Peter 3:9; Luke 13:1-5. Rev. 18:4; Rev. 22:17.

When the time comes, and we stand before Christ at the judgment seat; your name is called, and you walk forward to stand before the Creator, the Lord Jesus Christ, 2 Cor. 5:10: what will you say to Him when He asks you, what was your understanding of the law of His 4th Commandment? See in relation Luke 10:26. We must all give account of ourselves to God. Rom. 14:10-12. The judgment Jesus renders will be according to the will of the Father. John 5:27-30. Jesus says that in the day of His return many will question Him about their salvation. In Matt. 7:21-23, He says: "Not everyone that saith unto me, Lord, Lord, shall enter into the kingdom of heaven, but he that doeth the will of my father which is in heaven. Many will say to me in that day, Lord, Lord, have we not prophesied in thy name? And in thy name have cast out devils? And in thy name done many wonderful works? And then will I profess unto them, I never knew you: depart from me, ye that work iniquity." Iniquity is defined as sin, transgression of the law, fleshly desires, and evil works per biblical revelation. Rom. 1:18-32; 1 Cor. 6:9, 10; Gal. 5:19-21. By standing in opposition to the Commandments spoken by God Himself: where does your allegiance lie, and with whom do you align yourself with? Think about it!

Try to comprehend this, and understand it: With the words Jesus says that He will speak to those who commit lawlessness/iniquity/sin; depart from me, and I never knew you, let us examine the Sabbath covenant. See Exod. 31:13. God says for you to keep the Sabbath throughout your generations that you may know (have full assurance, understand, experience) that I am the Lord that doth sanctify you. (make you pure/holy) The condition is to keep the Sabbath that you may realize God is sanctifying you. If you are not there on His established day of rest, He cannot sanctify you according to His Word! Do you understand what you are missing out on? The example of disobedience was the Israelites while journeying through the wilderness. Because they did not obey the Sabbath precepts Moses preached unto them, they could not receive the covenant blessing God had promised, to bestow upon them.

Because the Word of the Lord endures forever, Isa. 40:8, nothing of all that God taught them has changed, it remains stedfast. The Sabbath rest remains, Heb. 4:9-11. All the blessings remain, Isa. 56:1-8; 58:12-14; Deut. 28:1-14. The holy convocation remains to be the 7th day, Lev. 23:1-3; Luke 4:16; 23:56; Mark 2:27; Acts 13:14-44; 15:21; 16:13,14; 17:2; 18:4; Heb. 4:1-11. Remember, under the covenant, one must appear before the Lord for sanctification on the 7th day Sabbath in obedience as a sign between God and you, Exod. 31:13, 17; and hold the Sabbath observance as a perpetual covenant, Exod. 31:16. This is why God told them to remember the Sabbath day to keep it holy because of the spiritual significance concerning it. To defile it or work on it was a certain death because it breaches the holiness of God, and it very well could be one of the reasons Jesus would say depart from me, you were not among my people in appearance on my holy day for sanctification and appropriation of holiness: "I never knew you." God's will is for man to keep convocation before Him on the 7th day. Lev. 23:3. God's call to worship is according to His word because He cannot lie, Heb. 6:18, and He said, "the 7th day is the Sabbath of the Lord thy God," Exod. 20:10. God desires you to revert back to the correct order of rest and worship in admonition to repentance. Rev. 14:6, 7. It is your duty to fear God and keep His Commandments. Eccles. 12:13. Jesus says, "except ye repent, ye shall all likewise perish." Luke 13:5. See 2 Pet. 3:9. Repentance is turning from sin, not remaining in it. Rom. 6:1-23. God will help you, trust Him. Prov. 3:5, 6; Rom. 10:13.

God requires your worship, Matt. 4:10; on the day He assigned for it, Lev. 23:3; from the foundation of the world, Gen. 2:1-3; which was created for man. Mark 2:27. The 7th day is the Sabbath of the Lord thy

God, Exod. 20:8-11; which remains for each believer to observe, Heb. 4:9-11; for the appropriation of holiness upon you. Exod. 31:13, see Heb. 12:14. According to the Holy Bible, each person will worship God by His established precepts, or will worship Satan in rebellion to the Word. This is a clear concept given in heavenly admonition to all of earth's population by angelic ministry of Rev. 14:6, 7, for God's worship by the word; or for Satan's worship in rebellion to God's established order of worship. Rev. 14:8-11. The call is to: "Fear God, and give glory to him; for the hour of his judgment is come: and worship him that made heaven, and earth, and the sea, and the fountains of waters." This direct warning is to heed the Mosaic establishment of Sabbath observance in worshipping God according to His Word. Rebellion to God's Word puts the wayward soul in opposition to Him, as is also the antichrist, the beast, and Satan; and is most likely they would worship the image of the best whose end is to be burned with fire and brimstone in the presence of the holy angels. Rev. 14:8-11. Do not remain in sin/rebellion, come out of it. Rev. 18:4. He that hath an ear, let him hear what the Spirit saith unto the churches. Rev. 3:22. The word of the Lord endureth forever, Isa. 40:8; 1 Pet. 1:25, literally forever. Ps. 119:152, 160; Ps. 33:11; Eccles. 3:14.

Chapter 12 –
The Spirit and
the Bride Say Come

After reading the Sabbath precepts, commands, and convocation: and you see that your life is in need of repentance, simply humble yourself and pray to God. Ask Him to forgive you, and confess your sins. 1 John 1:9. God does not want you to perish but have everlasting life, John 3:16. His desire for you is to come to repentance, 2 Pet. 3:9, and obey the Word. 1 John 2:1-6. The Lord is come to seek and to save those who are lost, Matt. 18:11.

With outstretched arms, the Master's plea is, "Come unto me, all ye that labour and are heavy laden, and I will give you rest. Take my yoke upon you, and learn of me; for I am meek and lowly in heart; and ye shall find rest unto your souls for my yoke is easy, and my burden is light." Matt. 11:28-30.

The Father's plea unto you is, "Seek ye the Lord while he may be found, call ye upon him while he is near: Let the wicked (Ps. 119:21) forsake his way, and the unrighteous man his thoughts: and let him return unto the Lord, (Ezek. 18:27, 28) and he will have mercy upon him (Jer. 29:12, 13, see Rom. 10:8-13); and to our God, for he will abundantly pardon." Isa. 55:6, 7; see Heb. 8:12; 2 Cor. 6:14-7:1. "Look unto me, and be ye saved (Ezek. 18:21-32) all the ends of the earth: for I am God, and there is none else. I have sworn by myself, the word is gone out of my mouth in righteousness, and shall not return, that unto me every knee shall bow, every tongue shall swear," Isa, 45:22, 23; in relation to Matt. 25:31-46; Rom. 14:10-12; John 5:28-30, Ps. 22:27, 28.

The call of the Holy Spirit is, "And the Spirit and the bride say, Come. And let him that heareth say, Come. And let him that is athirst come. And whosoever will, let him take the water of life freely." Rev. 22:17.

All people will stand before Jesus Christ either at the judgment seat of Christ, Rom. 14:10-12; or at the great white throne judgment, Rev. 20:11-15. When the angel record bearer calls your name, you will come and stand before the King of Kings. After the evaluation of your life is weighed in the balance and God's decision is rendered concerning your position either in His kingdom or against it, what would you rather hear from the King's mouth: "Well done, thou good and faithful servant: enter thou into the joy of thy Lord," Matt. 25:21; or, "Depart from me, ye cursed, into everlasting fire?" Matt. 25:41. Whoever's name is not written in the Lamb's book of life, will be cast into the lake of fire. Rev. 20:15. Those who call upon the name of the Lord shall be saved. Rom. 10:13, and those who are obedient shall eat of the tree of life. Rev. 22:14. While there is still time, you need to make the choice of life. Deut. 30:19, 20. And you should make the decision to serve the Lord. Josh. 24:15.

My personal advice is for you to take that step in faith to obey the command: "Remember the Sabbath day to keep it holy." Exod. 20:8-11. Change your life, obey God, and come to the 7th day holy convocation on the day God Himself blessed from the foundation of the world. Gen. 2:1-3; Lev. 23:3. Don't be just a hearer of the word, but be a doer of the word. That person will be blessed in his deed. James 1:22-25. Remember, God's blessing comes upon a person and overtakes him because he does what the Word says. Deut. 28:1, 2. See 3-14. God also promises blessing upon the faithful observer of His Sabbath. See Isa. 56:1-8; Isa. 58:12-14.

May you humble yourself and come with joy to the house of God to worship Him in spirit and in truth.

The Spirit and the Bride Say Come

John 4:23, 24, on the Sabbath convocation, Lev. 23:1-3, like Jesus did, Luke 4:16, like Paul did, Acts 17:2, being led by Christ in paths of righteousness as His namesake, Ps. 23:1, 2, by the Holy Spirit, John 16:13, into all truth. Jesus says, "He that hath an ear, let him hear what the Spirit saith unto the churches." Rev. 3:22, Amen. God richly bless you both now and forevermore.

In Jesus Christ,
James Madison McCauley 3rd

Sabbath Outline

Sabbath Revealed by Moses	Ps. 103:7; Neh. 9:13, 14
God's Rest	Gen. 2:1-3
Entering into God's Rest	Heb. 4:9-11
Sabbath Law, 4th Commandment	Exod. 20:8-11
Death: Penalty for working on it	Exod. 31:15
Scriptural Example	Num. 15:32-41
Death: Penalty for Defiling It	Exod. 31:14
Scriptural Example	Ezek. 20:1-21; 1 Cor. 10:1-11
Sabbath Refreshing	God, Exod. 31:17; man, Exod. 23:12
Sabbath Covenant	Exod. 31:12-17
Sabbath Holy Convocation	Lev. 23:1-3
Blessing for Observance, Gentile	Isa. 56:1-8
Blessing for Observance, House of Jacob	Isa. 58:12-14

Sabbath Rest Remains	Heb. 4:9-11
Jesus Christ's Custom	Luke 4:16
Followers Rest on Sabbath	Luke 23:56
Paul's Custom	Acts 17:2
Jews/Gentiles Convocation Observance	Acts 13:42-44
Sabbath Convocation when Scriptures Preached	Acts 15:21
Jesus Preaches on Sabbath Convocation,	Luke 4:16; Matt. 4:23 Matt. 9:35; 12:1-13; Mark 1:21; Mark 6:2; Luke 6:6
Paul Preaches on Sabbath Convocation,	Acts 17:2; 18:4; 13:14-44; 16:13
Sabbath Weekly Observance a Perpetual Covenant	Exod. 31:16
Sabbath a Sign Between God and Man Forever	Exod. 31:17

Sabbath of the Lord in all your Dwellings	Lev. 23:1-3
Restoration of Sabbath	Isa. 28:9-13; 58:12-14; Rev. 14:6, 7
Sabbath Observed in Convocation During Millennium	Ezek. 46:3
Sabbath Observed Forever in Eternity	Isa. 66:22, 23
7th Day Sabbath, "My holy day, the holy of the Lord"	Isa. 58:13
The Lord's Day	Rev. 1:10

About the Author

James Madison McCauley 3rd is a believer in the faith of our Lord Jesus Christ. As a child he and his family attended services at the Seventh-day Adventist Church on Patterson Avenue in Richmond, Virginia. He had attended the church school, Richmond Jr. Academy, from the 2nd - 8th grades before attending public schools as a teenager. At the age of 9, he accepted Jesus Christ as his Saviour, and was baptized into the faith by Elder McComas. He has loved God from an early age with the feeling of closeness to the Lord, even during adulthood. He is the father of a son, Rusty, and a daughter, Kathleen, who he loves dearly, which are now adults. During the late 80's he was called by the Holy Spirit to teach others about the 7th day Sabbath doctrine, and holy convocation. When he understood the Sabbath covenant,

Exod. 31:12-17, and the penalty for violating it, is when the Lord said unto him, "Son of man, give them warning from me." This book is the admonition of the Holy Sabbath and the convocation. God also gave him confirmation of his calling with a heavenly vision. One day he was sitting on his bed watching TV and the vision befell him. Total silence and not being able to know what was around him or hear the noise of the people around him befell him. He was in the Spirit and saw himself sitting in a pew on the right side in a church. As he looked toward the front, he saw a wooden alter with a cross on it. He looked to the top of it and there was a large opened Bible upon it. As he beheld the sight a hand appeared and started to flip through a few pages. When it stopped, the hand pointed to a verse of Scripture, and then it vanished. As he was wondering what the Lord had pointed at in the Bible, he looked up above the altar and a mouth appeared and it started to speak. He could see the teeth, the lips, and the tongue talking, but could not hear what was said by Him. As he sat there wondering what the Lord had said, he heard a voice behind him which spoke into his right ear. He said, "For with the stammering lips and another tongue will he speak to this people. To whom he said, this is the rest wherewith ye may cause the weary to rest; and this is the refreshing; yet they would not hear." Isa. 28:11, 12; see vs. 9-13. It is his prayer that by the grace of God, you will also come to understand this doctrine of the Sabbath, the covenant, and the convocation as appointed by God Himself. James has read the Bible for over 5 decades, and has completed various Bible correspondence courses. He has studied under Marilyn Hickey Ministries which is in Denver Colorado. His achievements are Mature Christian Living, and Victorious Beginning In Christ. Grace to you and peace from God our Father, His Holy Spirit, and our Lord Jesus Christ, Amen.

Synopsis

Jehovah created rest, Gen. 2:1-3; for the benefit of man, Mark 2:27. Jesus observed the Mosaic convocation, Lev. 23:1-3; Luke 4:16. Paul observed as tradition, the Levitical command, Acts 17:2. The Jews and Gentiles continue to hold the Sabbath convocation of the 7th day decades after the ascension of Jesus Christ, Acts 13:14-44; 17:2; 18:4. Change in the covenant occurred by man by promulgated law in 321 A.D. by Roman Emperor Constantine. God desires repentance, Isa. 58:12-14; the angelic call to worship the Creator, Rev. 14:6, 7. God's Sabbath covenant calls for observance throughout our generations, Exod. 31:12-17, and for all eternity, Isa. 66:22, 23. God is calling His people all over the world to come out of Babylon, Rev. 18:4, and obey His truths. The call of Christ is: "Repent: for the kingdom of heaven is at hand." Matt. 4:17. What will you do?

We invite you to view the complete
selection of titles we publish at:

www.ASPECTBooks.com

scan with your mobile
device to go directly
to our website

Please write or email us your praises, reactions, or
thoughts about this or any other book we publish at:

AB ASPECT Books
www.ASPECTBooks.com

Info@ASPECTBooks.com

TEACH Services, Inc., titles may be purchased in bulk for
educational, business, fund-raising, or sales promotional use.
For information, please e-mail:

BulkSales@ASPECTBooks.com

Finally if you are interested in seeing
your own book in print, please contact us at

publishing@ASPECTBooks.com

We would be happy to review your manuscript for free.